I Ain't Much To Look At . . .
But My Wife Is!

I Ain't Much To Look At . . . But My Wife Is!

A Man's Guide to a Long, Successful Marriage

Arnold E. Harner

Library of Congress Control Number: 2009904292
ISBN: Hardcover   978-1-4415-3405-7
                 Softcover   978-1-4415-3404-0

To order additional copies of this book, contact:
Xlibris Corporation
1-888-795-4274
www.Xlibris.com
Orders@Xlibris.com
61627

Contents

To my wife, Lisa, who has been my best friend for over thirty years.

Preface

FIRST OF ALL, let me say that I don't have an *MD, PhD, OG, or LMNOP* after my name. I'm just a regular fifty-something-year-old baby boomer who's been married to the same woman for almost thirty years. I've been with her for more years than that, and I can't imagine my life without her. I think that, along with a lot of research, qualifies me to share with you guys seven areas that I've found will make for a long and successful marriage.

If you're like most guys, you don't really care to read a lot (unless it's the pages of *Sports Illustrated* or *Playboy* for the articles), so I'll try to keep this entertaining and to the point. If you're in a serious relationship and ready to commit to the marriage scene, engaged, a newlywed, or been married for a while, I hope you'll find something helpful in these next few pages. Like I said, I'm not a psychiatrist, psychologist, therapist, or even a counselor, but I have interviewed hundreds of men and women – most of them married a minimum of twenty years – and compiled their results as well as my own thoughts in the pages of this book. I hope this collection of information and insight will help you on your life's journey with your wife, especially if you're still young. After all, it was Benjamin Franklin that said, "Life's tragedy is that we get old too soon and wise too late." When it comes to marriage, maybe you can develop wisdom quicker than I did. Life is a series of lessons, some we learn from to make our lives better, and some we don't. This book is full of commonsense ideas and strategies you can use to make your relationship with your wife (or future wife) so much better. There are a lot of tools at your disposal found in these pages; use them wisely and often. I'm not a genius, but I've tried to learn from my mistakes and from the wisdom of others. Common sense goes a long way to making life easier and to making marriages last. By the way, kudos to *Dr. Phil* for parlaying commonsense life's lessons into a multimillion dollar pot of gold!

> *Success is more a function of consistent common sense than it is of genius.*
>
> – An Wang (Wang Computers)

Chapter 1

Make Sure Your Wife is Your Best Friend

A friendship like love is warm; a love like friendship is steady.
                                                    – Thomas More

I BELIEVE THE "Free love, if it feels good do it" battle cry of the "me generation" is a bunch of crap. With the divorce rate peeking in 1981 with almost 53 percent of marriages ending in divorce, the "me first" mind-set hasn't worked out too well for us. However, according to *Divorce Magazine*, the divorce rate has been steadily declining since 1981. In 1990, it was 47 percent. In 2000, the divorce rate was 42 percent. And in 2005 the divorce rate had dropped to 36 percent. *Wow!* You're probably saying to yourself, "This is great. The divorce rate has fallen over the past twenty-five years from almost 53 percent to only 36 percent. What a great trend. People are actually staying married." In a way, you'd be right. But as Paul Harvey would say, "And now, the rest of the story." See, the thing is that the percentage of heterosexual couples who have *gotten married* has dropped in the last twenty-five years too.

What's the deal? Why aren't as many couples getting married? Well, we could blame it on a lot of things. One thing might be that growing up in a single parent or blended family home has something to do with it. A study done by Rutgers University in 2005 concluded that only about 63 percent of American children grow up with both biological parents. Sadly, this is the lowest rate in the Western world!

A lot of people who grew up, and those who are now growing up as children of divorce, tend to see *marriage* as a recipe for disaster. *Hollywood* has fueled the notion that "a little piece of paper doesn't make any difference; we're totally committed to each other." Well, as some of my friends would say, "That dog won't hunt." If what they say in *Hollywood* is true, why do people get married at all? That little piece of paper does make a difference, a huge difference, if you really want it to. Besides, we all know how well *Hollywood* commitments work out.

People who have grown up in homes where their parents were at each other all the time arguing, fighting, maybe even living through verbal and physical abuse have a real reason to be turned off by the thought of marriage. After all, why put yourself in a situation that may be almost impossible to get out of. My wife Lisa's story is a perfect example.

Lisa's childhood story of growing up in a *slightly* dysfunctional family was somewhat foreign to me when we first started dating. I grew up in a home where we weren't exposed to alcoholism, infidelity, and abuse. When my folks argued it was behind closed doors and usually when they didn't think we were around. If my mom and dad had friends that were going through the pain of divorce, we usually never knew about it till quite some time after the divorce was final. Lisa's childhood story was about to open my eyes to how a large, sometimes silent segment, of our population lives day to day. It's no wonder that so many people have such a dim view of the "bonds of matrimony."

As the second child of five children, Lisa grew up over a span of years when she observed her parents at their best, and at their worst. Her dad was in the army for a time and ruled his family with an iron fist. When he said "jump!" you didn't ask "how high?" you just started jumping. He would let you know if you were jumping high enough or not. He was the head of that family unit. He was the supplier, sustainer, and maintainer. For a long time, he worked hard and provided very well (monetarily) for his family. They were never really rich, but they were comfortable. Her mom took care of the house, helped with their business, and made sure Lisa's dad had whatever he needed. Their family business flourished. Weekend parties with their friends were the norm. I believe in the beginning that Lisa's mom and dad truly loved each other. They each filled a specific need that the other desired to have filled. Then, several years later, after a booming business that Lisa's father had built from the ground up collapsed, her dad really started drinking – a lot. Infidelity followed. Verbal, emotional, and to some extent, physical abuse crept into her parents' marriage. Through many years of torment though, her mom stayed married to her dad; after all, for a good Catholic girl, staying married was the only option. She dealt with a broken marriage day to day for many years till all of the kids were grown up and out of the house – then came the divorce. Too much water had passed under the bridge, too many hurtful things had happened, too much fatigue and exhaustion had set in to ever have what they thought was any hope of making a good marriage out of what they had left. It's no wonder that my best friend in the world almost ran away the day of *our* wedding. Lisa had grown up seeing a little of the best of her parents, but spent a whole lot of her childhood observing what a marriage should never be.

I hope that you find, as you read through this book, that your wife is to be cherished above every other earthly thing. If she sees that in you, it will add tremendous validity to those three little words every time you utter "I love you." Marriage is hard work, but it's also truly rewarding. We weren't designed to live this earthly life alone. That's why God created Eve, a friend for Adam.

Lisa and I attended the same high school in Florida. I was a year ahead of her, and even though we knew of each other, we ran around in different circles. After high school, we went different ways. I went away to college, and she started working full time. After a while I came back to Florida and started working at the same establishment as she did (this is where I do a plug for *Pizza Hut*). I'm sure the check's in the mail! Anyway, we got to know each other and started dating. We dated for two years. During that time, I must have asked her half a dozen times to marry me; every time, I got the same answer: "Maybe someday." I didn't give up. I didn't smother her, but I was persistent. It took her almost a year to tell me she loved me, so I was prepared to wait a while for the "Yes, I'll marry you." We were engaged for six months and were married July 26, 1980.

Now according to my research, not every successful marriage has a courtship that last two years. Some are longer, some are shorter. The secret is to spend time learning everything you can about your future wife. A few couples I've interviewed have been married over fifty years and only knew each other for a short time before they tied the knot. One couple only knew each other for a few weeks before getting married, but the odds of a marriage lasting such a long time after such a short courtship are slim at best.

Do you believe in love at first sight? I do. Love and marriage, however, are two different things. Take time to really get to know a woman (and I don't mean in the biblical sense). I'll explain my take on sex in a future chapter. Get to know what she really likes and dislikes. What kind of foods does she like. What's her least favorite food? Why? What's her favorite color? What does she like and dislike about her parents? (If she's truthful, they'll be a long list for both.) Does she want to have children? Can she even stand children? Are her grandparents still alive? What are they like? Questions about her education, where she grew up, what her childhood was like, and whether or not she beat up on her brothers and sisters, all make up who she is as a person. Lisa and I attended a wedding not too long ago where the engaged couple hadn't known each other very long. I hope and pray it works out for them, but after talking to the groom for a while, it was evident that we knew his new wife better than he did, and we've only known her a short time.

Masks

For thousands of years, masks were used to conceal the identity of the wearer. Figuratively, we all wear masks. We wear masks more often than we realize. We're constantly changing them depending on our particular situation. Part of our human makeup is to love and to be loved. We need to feel that people like us. That's oftentimes why we as guys try to be someone we're not, especially when meeting a woman for the first time. Whether we want to admit it or not, encountering a woman for the first time that we are obviously attracted to is pretty intimidating. Often, when we need to feel more comfortable seeking out a woman, we use the "wingman" approach. A "wingman" is a pilot who flies support for another pilot in a potentially dangerous environment, and believe me, the dating world is *definitely* a dangerous environment. The United States Air Force defines "wingman" in the traditional sense as the pattern in which fighter jets fly. When two fighter planes are airborne, there is usually a lead aircraft. The second aircraft flies just off the right wing and slightly behind the lead plane. Flying in this formation adds an extra pair of "eyes in the sky" and gives the pilot in the lead plane some comfort in knowing that his wingman has his back. In the dating world, we often use our wingman to gather intelligence for us. He's the one who brings us information about a potential mate. When we've deciphered all the intelligence that's been gathered, and have some idea of how to approach our "target," we then know what mask to wear to get the desired results. Now that's not to say that you can't get misinformation, bad intelligence or choose the worst mask possible to complete you mission (Lord knows I've crashed and burned more than once), but dating is a game of trial and error. You keep changing masks till you find one that works.

Wearing a mask may work for a while, but have you ever noticed that when you wear a real mask, even for a short time, it begins to get hot, scratchy, and downright uncomfortable? The same can be said for the figurative masks we wear. Every mask we wear is to cover up who we really are. Oftentimes we lie so much it becomes the truth to us. Have you ever heard someone say "he lies so much he can't keep his lies straight"? If you ever hope to achieve a lifelong relationship with someone who truly loves you for you, then grow up, throw the masks away, and be yourself. Your *wingman* can still be your friend, it's just that his job description may change a little. Eventually you and your *wife* will become *wingmates*, and with any luck and a lot of work, you'll be *wingmates* for life. A pilot trusts his wingman with his life, and that wingman usually knows his fellow pilot better than he knows himself. Get to really know your future wife before you get married. Figure out why she feels the way she does about marriage, children, family, and religion. Talk about her plans for the future and life in general. That way when life's little problems creep in to attack your marriage, you can be pretty confident that your *wingmate's* got your back.

For a lot of people (and I think just as many women as men), marriage is a very scary proposition. It doesn't take a rocket scientist to figure out that the problems that girls deal with growing up tend to shape their outlook of things that may be on the horizon for them as they become women. Common sense tells us that philosophy holds true for us men as well. If you grew up in a dysfunctional family and have a dim view of marriage, I understand, I really do, but consider breaking the cycle. Take a chance. You don't have to be your parents.

I guarantee you it will be a lot of work, but the rewards along the way are priceless. Make your wife your best friend!

> *I, not events, have the power to make me happy or unhappy today. I can choose which it shall be. Yesterday is dead, tomorrow hasn't arrived yet. I have just one day, today, and I'm going to be happy in it.*
>
> – Groucho Marx

Chapter 2

Pick Your Battles

Don't fight a battle if you don't gain anything by winning.

– General George S. Patton Jr.

H AVE YOU EVER heard the phrase "win the battle, but lose the war"? Learn to look at the big picture. Any time you win a small battle, but lose the war, it's what's called a "Pyrrhic victory." Pronounced (pĭr'ĭk), Webster's dictionary defines a Pyrrhic victory as "a victory or goal achieved at too great a cost." In 280 and 279 BC, King Pyrrhus of Epirus defeated the Roman armies at Heraclea and Asculum despite staggering losses to his own. This phrase was attributed to him in that even though he had won smaller battles against the Romans, one more *victory* could be the end of King Pyrrhus's army and his kingdom. So it is with married life. One of the secrets to a long marriage is knowing when to fight and when to take a loss (even when you know you're right) in order to preserve the sanctity and sanity of your marriage.

When I was a young newlywed struggling to assert my authority in our new home, Lisa and I had a few real *knock-down-drag-outs!* I knew I was right about certain things, and I wanted her to acknowledge it. Several times my ego overran my mouth, and I said some really stupid things. But then one day, I had a very wise old man asked me a question that I've never forgotten: "Would you rather be right or married?" Well, duh! "How did you get to be so smart?" I asked him. "Experience and common sense," he replied. "And usually common sense won't kick in before experience kicks me in the rear." Marriage is a series of ongoing battles of some kind. The trick is to come to the point where a lifelong truce is more highly prized than a string of wins.

Samuel Fuller said that "the creepy thing about battle is you always feel alone." When I fight with Lisa, I *never* (and I usually say . . . never say never), but really, I never feel better when I "win." Sometimes winning is a very lonely feeling. Society will tell you that "everybody loves a winner." But when the lights fade, and the cheers subside, you are once again all alone. Wouldn't it feel better to come in second place and have your wife hold you close when you slide under the covers? Or maybe you'd like to sleep on that friggin rock-hard couch another night! Pick your battles wisely!

> *Believe it or not, arguing is a form of communication. I didn't say it was a great form, but a form nevertheless.*

When it comes to battles, there are some family policies and procedures I'm not willing to budge on, and Lisa is the same. But over the years, we've learned exactly where the other stands on certain topics. When we start to get into an argument, I have to decide: Is this something open for discussion? Do I have any latitude in what I believe? Am I willing to suffer some repercussions for the stand I'm about to take? All of these questions have to be processed, sometimes in a matter of seconds, before my brain quits and my mouth engages.

Let's look at some reasons people *don't* stay married. The top five reasons are the following: financial issues; infidelity; communication breakdown; physical, psychological, and emotional abuse; and boredom. Although some of these issues are self-explanatory, let's look at finances for a minute. For me, when it's come to battles with Lisa, over the years, this one has been revisited several (hundred) times. Now with all the different levels that make up the pyramid of finances in a marriage, I need to decide which issues are small and which ones are major. A small issue for me is one of needing to know what personal items Lisa spends money on. As long as we can pay the bills on time, I really don't care to know what personal stuff she buys. If she wants a new pair of jeans or wants to donate money to a charity, it's all okay with me. I trust her to know if we can afford something or not. Now for some of you guys, this may be a major issue. Let me just say this. If your wife has never given you a reason to believe that she doesn't have the best interest of your family unit at heart, then take your pride, fold it up, and put it in your back pocket. Trust her with your finances until you have a reason not to. Lisa is a whole lot better with ours than I ever was. I bounced a rent check to our landlord (my mom's boss) after we had been married only two months. After that, Lisa was in control. Now it may be better for you the other way around. Talk about it before you get married.

For me, the idea of separate bank accounts is a major issue. I've always been a proponent of the "what's mine is yours and what's yours is mine" philosophy. I believe, and my research seems to back me up, the theory that everything we (as a married couple) have, earn, and hope to accumulate in the future belongs to both Lisa and me equally. I know that she will strive just as hard as I will to make sure that our basic needs and the needs of our family are taken care of. After that, if she wants something, hey, go for it. It makes me happy to see her happy. I trust her to use common sense, and it's worked out well so far. Your future wife may not be as good with money, but that's okay. Be smart. Work it out *before* you get married and keep in mind the following:

> *When your outgo exceeds your income, your upkeep will be your downfall.*

> – Bill Earle

There may have been a time in your life where irresponsibility in money matters has brought tremendous stress and suffering to a relationship very close to you, and I understand the fear of letting someone else have their fingers in your finances. A lot of people feel that *their money* is the only thing they have to fall back on if something happens in the relationship, but listen to me, nothing says *I love you* quite as loud as *I trust you* even with our money.

As I said before, even though I consider separate bank accounts to be a major issue for me, it's not a battle I would choose to lose the war over. In my mind I trust Lisa enough to know that if this is a battle she's willing to confront me with; then I will gracefully surrender. There are surely other battles to be fought, and if we as men can learn when to fight and when to surrender, we'll find it much easier to live in peace with our wives. Surrender doesn't mean you're weak; it just means that, for now, you've decided not to fight this particular battle.

Never misinterpret my silence as a sign of weakness.

– AH

Chapter 3

Change Your Definition of Love Along the Way: Phases of Marriage

When you're finished changing, you're finished.

– Benjamin Franklin

MOST EXPERTS AGREE that the majority of long-term marriages grow and evolve through four distinct stages. There is no particular time in a marriage when these stages occur (except the first) and at times they may overlap and become comingled.

The first is the *Romance and Honeymoon* stage.

My most brilliant achievement was my ability to be able to persuade my wife to marry me.

– *Winston Churchill*

All right, guys, settle down! This is the time, usually at the very beginning of the marriage, when all seems right with the world. Your new bride rushes home from work so she can make you your favorite dinner. She listens intently as you rant about what a crappy day you had and then with a kiss and a wink waves good-bye as you head out the door to shoot hoops with the guys. And in the back of your mind, you can still hear her sweet voice, whispering, "I've got a surprise for you when you get home!" Have you got it made or what! This marriage thing is awesome!

Of course now you just *have* to reciprocate. So the next day you send flowers to her work and all her friends just oooh and ahhh and tell her how she "married just the greatest guy ever." The honeymoon stage is a great phase to be in. You feel like love can conquer anything and that fifty years from now you and your wonderful bride will be sitting in your rocking chairs on the front porch watching the grandbabies play in the yard. In this phase, you do a lot for each other. You spend a lot of time talking on the phone (or *texting* each other). You possibly go out to lunch and dinner often, and the physical and sexual attraction is quite strong. This phase is oftentimes an extension of your courtship. You will do well to keep at least parts of this stage wound through the fibers of your marriage no matter how long it lasts.

> *A happy marriage has in it all the pleasures of friendship, all the enjoyments of sense and reason, and, indeed, all the sweets of life.*
>
> – Joseph Addison

The second is the *Reality* stage.

> *What is easy is seldom excellent.*
>
> – Samuel Johnson

There are a lot of people that define this stage as "the beginning of the end." It's really not; it's just another phase in your marriage walk. Remember, your marriage is what you make it. It's defined by the amount of work you're willing to put into it and whether the expectations you have are fulfilled or not. So if you prepare for this stage ahead of time and realize that it is going to be a part of your marriage journey, you're much more likely to have just choppy waters instead of a tsunami.

It's in this phase of the marriage that you really start to learn more and more about your wife. You learn things like the following: What makes her snore like a freight train? Does she really like a clean house, or is she a proverbial slob? Does she want children of her own, or is she happier babysitting for your friends and shipping the little brats home? Did she really want to marry you, or does she think she made a mistake? Of all the questions you may ask of each other, this is probably the scariest. It's scary for guys partly because we as men hate to lose. We hate to lose at anything. The wedding itself is like our Olympic podium. It tells everybody that we came, saw, and conquered; and if our marriage ends in divorce, it's like our victory's been overturned and we have to give our medal back. We as men usually spend a lot of time, money, and energy in the courting process, and the wedding is the culmination of that whole process. The same can probably be said by our wives. They have a lot invested in us, and whether we want to admit it or not, we've been conquered too.

It's probably safe to say that for most of us, we were not our wife's first boyfriend; and if we're honest, we were probably not our wife's first serious relationship. If our marriage ends in divorce, this loss puts us in the same category as all the other guys who have lost; and all the sudden, when it comes to having this wife, we're not special anymore. Losing sucks! After all, who remembers who came in second in the 1976 Olympic decathlon? Nobody! I'll bet you know who took home the gold though. That's right – Bruce Jenner. Enough said. By the way, just for future reference so you can impress your buddies, it was Guido Kratschman from Germany who took home the silver that same year.

But now the wedding's over, and your wife's not the center of attention anymore. Your friends give you a hard time, complaining that they don't see you enough. Arguments with your wife are more frequent than ever and are over the stupidest things. At times (usually during a heated argument) you even question why you got married. Sex is sporadic and routine at best. You never can seem to be on the same schedule. By now you may have kids, and that in and of itself has it's own set of challenges. You thought after you were married, she would change. Little things she does that you used to think were cute now drive you crazy! Remember, these feelings are normal. I didn't say good, just normal. But if you are prepared for this stage and ready to give like you have never given before, you can make it through this part of your marriage with flying colors (or minimal scarring) however you want to look at it.

This stage is so very challenging. Statistics show that the first two years of your marriage have the highest risk of encountering an affair or worse, divorce.

Don't be scared, be prepared. Learn to compromise!

Better to bend, than to break.

– Old Scottish Proverb

The third stage is the *Rediscover, Reacquaint, and Reconnect* stage.

A friend is a gift you give yourself.

– Robert Louis Stevenson

After you've had some time (usually years, even decades) to work through the reality stage, you will eventually move into this third stage. This time of rediscovery, reacquainting, and reconnecting usually starts to take place about the time your children are in their late teens to early twenties. It's about the time they leave home to be on their own in college, working, and searching for their own wives (or husbands if you have daughters). It's at this time in a marriage when your wife – and to some degree, you – may start to show symptoms of "the empty-nest syndrome." This may be a rough time for her. Give her some special attention. Comfort her. Do unexpected little things for her. Remember when you were dating? Remember the "Romance" stage? It's time you made time to do things that you both enjoy. Buy her flowers for no special reason. Drop in and take her to lunch. Get home early and make her favorite dinner. And this one will get you more points than just about anything: Take off a day from work without telling her. Sneak home and clean the whole house! I mean *clean*, from the dishes to the laundry, from the bedroom to the bathroom. Now I know some of you feel brutally emasculated right now like you just lost your two best friends (if you know what I mean), but trust me, this will get you more miles than you can imagine. You will be "The Man."

Set aside one night a week for "date night"; one night when it's just the two of you. You go out to dinner, maybe a movie, maybe to the mall. Maybe you'll want to take her to a ball game; go bowling; or possibly take a blanket, find your favorite parking spot, and lay out under the stars. The point is to spend at least one night a week focused on what the two of you like to do together. A typical "date night" for Lisa and me is to go out some place nice for dinner (it doesn't have to be expensive) and then we go do the grocery shopping at Wal-Mart. Sounds romantic, right? Well, we don't especially love spending time at Wal-Mart, but it's something we do together, just the two of us.

In this stage, it's very important that you put a lot of emphasis on what makes you and your wife happy. Hopefully you've figured out through the years that you are truly different people with different views, interests, and talents. But if you've paid attention and learned over the years, you know how to take the best of what you are and combine it with the best of what your wife is to make a great team. You've also learned to compromise in your differences. Take this time to get to know each other all over again: to rediscover what it was that attracted you to each other, to get reacquainted with the girl you fell in love with, and to reconnect to each other in little ways that are truly meaningful.

> *A successful marriage requires falling in love many times, always with the same person.*
>
> – Anonymous Quote

The last stage is the *Success* stage.

Remember that these stages appear at different times and overlap at different points in each couple's marriage. This is the stage that is probably the most intimate and rewarding.

> *Love seems the swiftest, but is the slowest of all growths. No man or woman really knows what perfect love is until they have been married a quarter of a century.*
>
> – Mark Twain

Now you've made it! When you get to this stage of your marriage, you've just about seen and lived it all. You and your lovely bride have been through a lot of ups and downs, some struggles small, some extremely large.

I remember New Year's Day 1983. I went on a day-long deep-sea fishing trip off the coast of Fort Pierce, Florida, with my dad, brother, and brother-in-law. We left the docks early. The trip started out nice enough. We had blue skies, and it wasn't too hot. The skipper took us out about seven miles from shore to what he thought was a good spot to fish. The only problem was the fish didn't get the directions to where we were gonna be. After a few hours and very few bites, he made the decision to take us out twenty miles to the Gulf Stream where he just knew the fishing would be better. Well, the fishing was better, and we were having a great time till about 2:00 p.m. We could see dark clouds closing in on us from the south. The skipper got on the radio, and sure enough, a squall line was headed our way. There wasn't much chance of outrunning the storm, but he was going to try. We pulled everything in and packed up as quickly as we could, then headed for shore. It was the worst two-hour boat ride of my life. Now I'm not sure why we chose to take tuna salad sandwiches and sardines with crackers for lunch but – bad idea! I never really had an iron stomach, more like a paper-bag design, and buddy was it put to the test. We were riding eight-to-ten-foot swells on what felt like a piece of plywood. Trust me, tuna salad tastes much better going down than it ever did coming up!

The point is that some of the ups and downs of a marriage are like riding eight-to-ten-foot swells on a piece of plywood twenty-five miles off the Florida coast in the middle of the Atlantic Ocean. Some times you're sick and tired, and you wonder if you should have ever ventured out. But just as sure as we made it back to the docks at Ft. Pierce, you have made it through some very tough storms in your marriage. When you finally get to this stage, you and your wife have a deep, profound love that has weathered the storms of life, not without some nausea and pain, but you made it through just the same.

Your wife knows you better than you know yourself. She's seen you as a man at your best, and your worst. When you finally arrive at this stage, sex may still be sporadic but is probably far from routine. You'll find yourself more intimately focused on the emotional needs of your wife, and she on yours. You find yourself thinking about all the good times and the struggles you've made it through together, and you won't be able to imagine your life without her. This is the stage all of us long to reach. Believe me, you'll know when you get here. By the way, don't forget to continue to incorporate the *Honeymoon* stage. You'll both get a kick out of it!

Those who love deeply never grow old; they may die of old age, but they die young.

– Benjamin Franklin

Chapter 4

Buckle Up! Mother Nature's About to Visit!

Don't think of it as getting hot flashes . . . think of it as your inner child playing with matches.

– Maxine

NOW THE CHAPTER you've been waiting for. In this chapter we'll deal with biology, hormones, virgins, and sex. I told you earlier in this book that we would discuss the topic of sex, but don't skip over the first part of this chapter or you'll miss some really important stuff. In order to know your wife better, you need to know what she constantly has to deal with physically, mentally, and emotionally. My wife, Lisa, has made a certain comment to me on more than one occasion, and it goes something like this: "I wish you had to, just once, go through what I go through every month." Of course I blow it off because I lump it in with the other completely unfounded "women can endure much more pain than men" theory. Then I tell her, "That's just something all women say 'cause they know we can't call your hand on it." Then I started reading up on all the physical and hormonal changes women go through for an average of 85 percent of their lives! I'm so glad I'm a man, and you should be too. The more I learn about women, the more I think that Eve may have gotten the short end of the stick during the punishment phase in the *Garden of Eden* trial.

Let's take a look for a second at just the physical hoops women have to jump through. Between the ages of ten and sixteen and at an average age of twelve or thirteen, a girl begins to become a woman. Girls and women get to deal with the menstruation (from the Latin *menses*, which means "month") cycle. I know, I know, I hate talking about it too, but the more you know about what a woman has to deal with, the more you can empathize with her when that time comes. I cringed for years when Lisa would ask me to go to the grocery store and pick up a "package" for her on aisle 2. Not just any package, oh no. It had to be a specific brand; certain color wrapper; specific size; with or without wings; for light, medium, or heavy days; twelve or twenty-four count; and on and on. Lord, help me, if they were out of that one; then I'd have a whole new list of things to look for. Why can't they be like oil filters? You go into an auto parts store, tell the guy which vehicle you have with what engine, and, boom, you've got two maybe three filters to pick from, and they all work pretty much the same! But, no, I have to stand in the same spot on aisle 2 for ten minutes looking like a caveman without a clue. I think there's a Bible reference for this situation found in the book of John: "Greater love has no man than this, that he would spend his time searching for items on aisle 2 for his wife." This single act of unconditional love should speak volumes to your wife about how much you care for her!

All right, back to biology. Almost all women have what's called a *uterus*. There are always exceptions to everything, but 99.9 percent of all women have one. It's the place inside a woman where a baby is formed and develops. The uterus has a lining that, monthly, gets thicker in preparation for a fertilized egg to grow. If the egg isn't fertilized, the uterus sheds this thick lining and returns to normal. This time of her menstruation is when we consider her to get her *period*. A woman loses about thirty to forty milliliters of blood and around eighty-five to ninety milliliters of total fluid during that three-to-ten day period. Remember, this usually happens every single month!

There you have it: a brief biological explanation of a woman's menstruation period. But wait, if that's not enough to go through, there are hormonal swings that occur to bring about these biological changes. When a baby girl is born, she normally has two ovaries. By the time she reaches puberty, each ovary still has about two hundred thousand eggs left in it – four hundred thousand eggs! Can you imagine? Can't relate? Try this: if every egg was the size of a regulation-size MLB baseball bat, there would be enough bats to fill up Noah's Ark! Still can't quite picture it? How about enough baseball bats to fill up 522 standard railcars! That's a lot of bats, or eggs. Not all of these eggs are viable for reproduction. Normally, only about five hundred or so will be available for fertilization during a woman's reproductive years. If you figure a woman's menstruation period last twenty days, that's thirteen periods a year. Thirteen periods a year over a thirty-eight to thirty-nine year reproductive life span is right around five hundred eggs.

There are two major female hormones that regulate a woman's period, *estrogen* and *progesterone*. *Estrogen* and *progesterone* levels fluctuate wildly every month depending on what part of her cycle a woman is in and whether or not the egg she is carrying is fertilized. She goes through all of this every twenty-eight days just to prepare her body for the chance that she may get pregnant. If she does get pregnant, then the baby requires the mother's body to produce another whole new level of hormones to add to the estrogen/progesterone club, and things really start to get weird. Can you imagine? Nine months of hormone levels raising and lowering to support not only her life, but also sustaining the new life growing inside her too? Then after the baby's born, everything's supposed to go back to normal quickly like nothing happened. Easy, right? I don't think so.

Now after about forty years of monthly fluctuating hormone levels, we come to the historical moment in a woman's life known as *menopause*. Menopause, literally translated from the Greek, means a halt to the month. It designates the permanent end of a woman's menstruation. Menopause is proceeded by a year of *peri,* or *pre* menopause. It is at this particular time in your life when you as a man (if you play your cards right) may apply for sainthood! This time of her life will probably really be stressful for your wife; and because of the role you play in her life, guess what, it's gonna be stressful on you too! No one can tell when menopause occurs until after it has already happened. Let me explain how this works. Menopause signifies the end of fertility in a woman's life. When it occurs naturally in her life, she can't be defined as menopausal until her periods stop completely. When that happens for a span of twelve consecutive months, then she is considered to be in *postmenopause*. If, however, at any time during that twelve-month span she has a period or even any spotting, then she's not considered to be in menopause, and the twelve-month count starts all over again. So you see a specific date can't be assigned till after the fact, and it's hard to calculate a specific date. What's not so hard to figure out though is when the premenopausal time is occurring. In the United States, the average age of a woman in menopause is about fifty. Premenopause signs and symptoms usually occur about age forty to forty-five but can sometimes show up as early as age thirty-five. A woman's premenopausal years are probably the most confusing for us guys. Imagine what it must be like for a woman. Why is premenopause, menopause, and postmenopause such a stressful time for us as men? Think about that week or so before your wife has her period. That time when you usually walk on eggshells and try very hard not to make any waves. Now multiply that feeling by one hundred and try to guess which month, week, or day it's gonna hit. You'd have a better chance of winning a multimillion dollar lottery two months in a row! Now I love Lisa to death, but there were nights during her premenopausal years when I hid all the kitchen knives and slept with one eye open! I not only had to watch what I said, but also how I said it and who I said it to! But I had to keep telling myself that this wasn't the girl I married. I mean it was, but because of all the physical and emotional changes brought about by changes in her chemical and hormonal levels, Lisa was *at times* a different person. I had to remind myself that menopause signaled the end of her reproductive years. There is a strong fluctuation in a woman's hormone levels that rivals those of her teenage years, just in reverse. At the beginning of puberty, a woman's hormone levels swing wildly to prepare her body for childbearing. At menopause, they swing wildly to "gear down" a woman's body when reproduction is no longer a natural option. Some of you may say, "But my wife's had a hysterectomy, surely she's in menopause now." The truth is that even though she may not have her uterus anymore, as long as she still has one ovary that is functioning, releasing reproductive hormones, she can't be considered menopausal. If, on the other hand, her ovaries are removed but she still has her uterus intact, she is immediately considered to be in "surgical" menopause. This is often the hardest type of menopause for a woman to deal with.

Unlike natural menopause, her body has no time to prepare for what's about to happen. If she goes through surgical menopause (the removal of her ovaries and fallopian tubes) she will have an extreme and total drop in female hormone levels, which will produce drastic hormone withdrawal symptoms. These can include, but are not limited to, hot flashes, itching, dryness, joint pain, back pain, muscle pain, mood swings, irritability, fatigue, poor night's sleep, memory loss, depression, and decreased libido (that's sex drive to you and me). I don't care who you are; that's a lot to deal with. Lisa went through a few years of premenopause before she found out that for health reasons she was about to endure "surgical" menopause. My wife is a stronger person than I am. Maybe there is something to the theory that women can deal with pain better than men!

Guys, please, I know it's not in our nature, not in our genetic makeup to be sympathetic and nurturing, but please try to get a handle on what your wife is going through. Show her the compassion and understanding she deserves. She deals with a lot of the same day-to-day problems you do and then has all this female stuff piled on top of that! The truth be told, after dealing with the *cycle* for years before you became a couple, she probably can tell when she's being oversensitive, cranky, and downright mean. But instead of whining and becoming defensive, suck it up, help with the dishes, the kids, and the laundry. I know it will help her, and it won't hurt you either!

Sex and Virgins

Marriage has many pains, but celibacy has no pleasures.

– Samuel Johnson

Okay, we're finally here. We're to the part of the book you've had to wade through the first four and a half chapters to get to. I told you we would eventually get here, but it may not be quite what you expected. Although after reading this, you may think I'm old-fashioned and a borderline prude, that's okay. I still believe that sex is something to be enjoyed by a man and a woman after they're married. I know, I know, you want me to step into the twenty-first century, but let me explain why I feel the way I do. First of all, let me say that if you are single and still a virgin, congratulations. Don't be embarrassed. Do you realize how special your wife will feel on your wedding night knowing that you've saved yourself for her and only her? Let me add this too: if you've had premarital sex, there's no crime in stopping now in anticipation of your wedding night. After all, for most guys, what special significance does making love with your wife on your wedding night have if you just slept with her a couple of days ago? Here's another thought: How anxious are you to have your lovemaking skills compared to another guys? Maybe not just compared to one other guy, but maybe two, three, or ten other guys! And how would you feel about being with a girl that can say she can compare you to a lot of other guys? Here's the harsh truth. If a guy sleeps with a lot of girls, he's experienced; if a girl sleeps with a lot of guys, she's a slut. It's been the same old double standard for thousands of years. I didn't say it was fair, it just is what it is. How great would it be to know that on your wedding night, your beautiful bride has saved herself for you and you alone. Some of you might say, "Hey, if I slept with other women, then my wife could appreciate all the techniques I've learned." Trust me, after you're married, you'll have plenty of time to practice; and with a little instruction from your wife, you'll have all the *technique* you need! Plus, if you both stay virgins till your wedding night, then you won't have to worry about those nasty little STDs, or worse yet, sexually transmitted AIDS creeping into your honeymoon bed. Lisa and I were both virgins when we got married; not that it was easy to wait two-and-a-half years while we were dating, but the honeymoon classes and homework were a lot of fun! I know . . . too much information.

Guys, you have to realize that for most women, the act of making love is very emotional as well as physical. For centuries, women have been taught that what they have is very special and no one should give it away freely. Women need to feel that what they are giving up to a man he cherishes because he loves her. The problem is that once she gives herself to a man, there is no taking it back. There is and always will be only one first time. Let me tell you, guys, if you really love her, you can wait for her. Don't make her feel obligated or guilty if she wants to wait till her wedding night to have sex, even if it's not with you. Every time you make love, or have sex (there is a difference), with a woman, there is an emotional bond that forms. They may all be on different levels, but at least in a woman's mind, there is some kind of bond nonetheless. For most guys, one-night stands and even casual sex is nothing more than a sexual-pressure release. Do we as men realize how that can affect the female psyche? How would you feel if you knew a guy used your sister for sex and then moved on to someone else? You'd want to rip his head off, right? How would you feel if your sister dated a guy for years – you knew they were having sex – then one day he decided to just move on to someone else? You'd want to rip his head off, right? Because she's your sister – now you're emotionally involved. Think about that the next time you feel that your girlfriend's not meeting your "needs."

Let's think about children for a second. There are thousands of unplanned pregnancies every year in the United States alone. There's a whole new mountain to climb, especially if you're not married. Of course, there are options. The woman can have the baby alone and become a single parent. She could have the baby then put it up for adoption. The couple could get married and raise the baby together, or abort the baby all together. Any one of these scenarios would be emotionally draining to say the least. I was one of the lucky ones. I'll share my story with you a little later in this book. Again, if you've never been married and are still a virgin, congratulations! You've proven what a strong person you are. Your virginity is something you can be proud of. It's something you can claim that sets you apart from the crowd, and if the crowd is really honest with themselves, it's something most of them wish they had saved for their own wedding night.

For every excuse you can throw out there to have sex, I can give you ten reasons not to. Wherever you are in your dating relationship, just sit back and be patient. I know it's not easy, but you can make it! Talk to your future wife about when you want to have children. Talk about how many kids you want to have and who will play what role in their upbringing. Even though I may sound like an overly sensitive and caring guy, I have to tell you I didn't have much to do with the day-to-day raising of our son until he got out of what I like to call "the possum stage." I didn't do many feedings and even less diaper changing, but Lisa and I both knew that going in, and he turned out to be a pretty good young man, if I do say so myself. When it comes to sex and biology, keep these three things in mind: Number one, remember that, especially for a woman, sexual intimacy is almost always more than physical. Number two, never pressure a woman in any way for sex. The act of making love forms an emotional bond. And number "C", keep in mind that if she seems moody and shares certain characteristics with serial killers, it probably has to do with chemical and hormonal changes you and I just can't imagine!

> *I blame my mother for my poor sex life. All she told me was the man goes on top and the woman underneath. For three years my husband and I slept in bunk beds.*
>
> – Joan Rivers

Chapter 5

Give the Gift That Keeps on Giving:
Love and Laughter

Laugh and the world laughs with you, weep and you weep alone.

– Ella Wheeler Wilcox

I 'M NOT SO sure I totally agree with this quote. Marriage should be a lifelong partnership where you always have someone willing to stand beside you and you beside her, in the good times and the bad. However, a marriage will be much happier if the weeping comes from tears of joy.

Did you know that laughter is not only good for your marriage, but it's good for your health too. In recent medical studies, it's been found that laughter actually helps your blood vessels function better. When you laugh, it causes your blood vessels to expand and contract, increasing blood flow and actually exercising the little fellas. One study done at the University of Maryland reported that laughing on a regular basis was as beneficial as aerobic exercise! As much as I laugh, I should be ready for an "Ironman Triathlon," but, hey, who are we kidding? Now I'm sure that the folks at UM would never want you to replace regular exercise with laughter, but laughing can't hurt. Laughter reduces pain. It lowers blood glucose levels in diabetics. It also helps us cope with elevated stress levels. Have you ever noticed that when you've had a rough day at work and you come home exhausted and tense, how the smallest funny comment from your child can almost immediately start to melt away the stress? It's almost impossible to be angry when you're laughing! Maybe you've got a favorite comedy TV show that helps you unwind. For me, my favorite movies are comedies. And as Lisa would say, "The dumber the better." When I want to relax, I want to be entertained and not have to think a lot. I want to laugh and loosen up. Of all my favorite top-ten movies, the top seven are all comedies. Come on, admit it: who doesn't bust out laughing or at least crack a smile when they recall the dinner table scene in Eddie Murphy's *The Nutty Professor*? Or grin when you think about Shake 'n Bake from *Talladega Nights*? Laughter really is beneficial to your health.

What soap is to the body, laughter is to the soul.

– Yiddish Proverb

When I was a kid growing up in Florida, one of the few things I really enjoyed reading was *Reader's Digest*. Of course the magazine was great each month, but there were a few sections I always flipped to first. If I didn't get a chance to read anything else there was always "Laughter, the Best Medicine," "Quotable Quotes," "Life in These United States," and "Humor in Uniform." I could always count on everything from grinning to laughing my butt off every time I read those few pages.

But life can't be humorous all the time. I've often wondered how people who have high-stress jobs deal with the same stuff as the rest of us after they've put in eight, ten, twelve, or more hours where you would be hard-pressed to think that laughter invades much of their day. How can they come home to their wives and husbands, relax and have fun, laugh and enjoy each other with the stress of the day looming over them? My mom spent almost all of her adult life in the health care profession as a nurse. She did everything from working in mental hospitals to administering chemotherapy to cancer patients. My sister Becky has devoted her life to nursing too. She's done everything from ER nursing to currently working with families and terminally ill patients in the hospice field. I've got a friend who's a fireman and a brother-in-law who's a paramedic. I've got a buddy who's had a successful career in law enforcement and is now captain of an elite SWAT team. How do people in these kinds of jobs cope? It's hard enough to work a normal nine-to-five job and then come home and deal with all the other stuff that goes into not only keeping a marriage together, but also making it good. I can't imagine having an emotionally charged job, dealing with life-and-death decisions all day long and then come home and deal with a spouse, kids, bills, and just life in general. So I thought, why not go to the source? Why not go to all these different people and find out exactly how they do it.

To tell you the truth, when I was young, I really wasn't aware that my mom may have had a stressful job. I was way too involved with my favorite person – me! But, recently, when she explained to me what she used to do to relax, a light came on and I remembered a lot of the things she did. I just recalled them as "the fun things we did." She reminded me that first of all she tried to separate her work life from her home life. She tried her best to never debrief the family about work-related topics. To help herself lighten up, she used to sew, ride her bicycle, and go bowling with my dad. She also immersed herself in politics and shuttling me along with my brother and sister to band practice, sporting events, and every place else we could talk her into taking us. But I think, more than anything else, she enjoyed relaxing with family and friends, people she could get close to and laugh with. I remember a lot of Saturday nights spent at the homes of my mom and dad's friends. All of us kids were usually busy doing something in the living room until we heard our moms and dads laughing. Then we would run over each other to get to the kitchen to see what was so funny.

My sister Becky deals with the stress in her job in a little different way. She likes to exercise to release physical stress and what she likes to call "laughing at yourself" to relieve emotional stress. She says you need to try to find humor in just about everything, even yourself! She told me a story of her early nursing career when she was working in the ER of a particular hospital in Florida. An elderly Seminole Indian woman had passed away on Becky's shift. The local medicine man had been in and performed the "last rites." A multitude of thoughts were swirling around in Becky's head as well as some mental images of a recent horror movie. Was all this a trick? Was she being "punked"? In a flash, would this woman sit straight up? Would she reach out and grab Becky's hand? She really started to get uncomfortable when the nurse that was with her was going to leave the room and asked Becky to place the elderly woman's dentures back in her mouth as they got her body ready to go home. Well, you can guess what happened. The other nurses heard Becky's panicked scream and came bolting back to the room. Even though it wasn't too funny at the time, all the nursing staff and my sister got a good laugh out of it later.

My buddy on the SWAT team says that the team is constantly playing practical jokes on each other. It helps to break the tension and relieve the stress of their job. The same holds true for my friend that's a fireman. My brother-in-law, the paramedic, is a real clown anyway. He has a gift for finding humor in almost anything. The common thread that runs through all of these people with high-stress jobs is laughter, and this special thread should also be found woven through your marriage. Like I said earlier, it's hard to stay angry if you're laughing. Laugh with your wife. Set aside time to do fun things with her. Remember a time when you laughed so hard you cried? Maybe so hard your sides hurt? Or maybe so hard you lost all, you know, bladder control? Come on, you know you did! Make those moments happen in your marriage; well, maybe not the bladder control thing. I'm definitely the clown in our marriage. I try to make Lisa laugh at least half a dozen times a day. Whether it's a funny story I heard at work, something I saw on the Internet, or just making a stupid funny comment about nothing, laughter just makes us feel better. Laughter enables us to lower our guard and feel closer to others. In laughter, we share a common bond. Now obviously, at times I've shared something with Lisa that I *thought* was funny, but it became apparent very quickly that we were not on the same page and she was *not* amused!

Here is something that you men will hopefully learn earlier than I did: know when to use your humor and charm on your wife and when to keep your trap shut! After all, it's hard to put your foot in your mouth if your lips aren't moving. But hey, everybody's different, and every couple is different. Just remember, laughter breaks down walls. When we're angry, we tend to immediately throw up a barrier. We become defensive and either want to fight or we clam up and internalize our anger. If though, through the use of laughter, we can relax and bring that anger level down, chances are that we can then start to discuss in a rational manner what exactly is bothering us.

I hope that one day, when I leave this earth for my new home, people will remember that I was fun to be around. That I would always make them laugh. That my friends and family would recall all the good times we had together. That Lisa could think back and reminisce about how I could make her smile even after a bad day. Let's face it. No matter what stresses the world throws at you, humor can help you cope with life. Give your family a legacy of love and laughter. It's not too late to start. Love and laughter, they go hand in hand.

> *Laughter is the lifeboat in humanity's stormy seas . . . love, the lighthouse.*
>
> – AH

Chapter 6

Don't Make Your Wife a Single Parent!

There are no illegitimate children – only illegitimate parents.

– Leon R. Yankwich

NOT MUCH ELSE will make your wife feel more alone and unloved than if she feels like she's raising children by herself. Like I said at the end of chapter 4, I was a pretty lucky kid. I was adopted by a loving couple when I was about two years old. Here's a little background to my story from information given to me by my adopted parents, my biological parents, and from what little bit I personally remember. My biological dad was in the military and stationed near Blercourt, France. That's where he met and married my mom. They dated for just a couple months. She was sixteen, and he was eighteen when they got married. My grandparents didn't like my dad at all, but my mom was ready for a better life in America. They were married for thirty-nine years till my dad passed away at age fifty-seven. I have two older brothers that were born in France. My dad was shipped back to the States, but it took over a year of trudging through red tape for my mom's papers to clear so she could come to the United States. I was the first of the original five children to be born here. After I was born, my mom and dad finally had a little girl.

Now for years my dad had been a social drinker, but after a while, he began to drink a lot. He would get liquored up and leave my pregnant mom with the four kids as he went on a three-or-four-day binge. Then he would come back home and work till he disappeared again the next weekend. One weekend while he was gone, my mom went into labor with child number five. There she was at home with four kids ranging from six years old down to a one year old. Her water had broken and there was no one there to help her. The neighbors didn't speak any French, and my mom spoke very little English, but they did manage to get her to the hospital in time. The language barrier became even more of a problem when my mom got to the hospital. The staff couldn't communicate with her, and as hard as they tried, they couldn't locate my dad to serve as an interpreter. After a couple of days, they sent her home with my newborn baby brother. Now my mom had five children under the age of six to care for on her own. If all that wasn't enough, a new complication arose. Within thirty-six hours from arriving home with my new baby brother, my mom started hemorrhaging. She was bleeding badly, and again, no dad around. This time the neighbors called an ambulance, and Mom was rushed to the hospital. The surgeons got the bleeding stopped, but it was then that the doctors and staff realized that something more than patching her up and sending her home had to be done. But what could they do? With their hands virtually tied, the staff called in the State of Florida's Child Services Division. The social worker did what she thought was best to help my mom. She convinced her to keep the oldest son and the baby boy but to let them take the three of us in the middle and put us in foster care until my dad could straighten out and get his life together. My mom agreed, and my older brother, younger sister, and I were headed to three different foster homes.

Foster care is okay as a stopgap measure, but it's not intended to be a way of life for any child.

Too many children in foster care are falling through the cracks . . .
Be a hero . . . take time to learn about adoption today.

– Bruce Willis

The older I get, the more I realized that there is a reason for everything. My adoptive mom and dad tried for years but just couldn't have any children of their own, so by the time I turned two, I had a new family. One of the really great things about this story though is that by the time my adoption went through, my new mom found out she was pregnant, and before long, I had a new baby sister. I guess this was sort of a confusing time for me though. I called my new sister by my biological sister's name, and any words I said to my new family were in French! But as I said, I was one of the lucky ones. I ended up with a wonderful mom and dad, who I love very much. I have a great sister and brother. I grew up in a caring home where I wanted for nothing and was accepted and loved. I always knew I was adopted. My mom and dad told me that they chose me out of all the other boys and girls they saw. That always made me feel special, but there are a lot of children that never get to share in that feeling. Maybe they're born in to a family where they're not wanted. Maybe they're being raised by a single mom, struggling to make it through the day. Maybe they're being raised by grandparents who never thought that at their age they would have children to raise again. Maybe they will grow up through the foster-care system. Maybe they didn't even have a chance to be born.

Here's my plug for adoption: If abortion was as easily accepted as a form of birth control fifty years ago as it is today, I may not exist. Here's a list of famous adopted people you may recognize:

Charles Dickens, Crazy Horse, Daunte Culpepper, Faith Hill, Dave Thomas (founder of Wendy's), Halle Berry, Mark Twain, Marilyn Monroe, Eric Dickerson, Jim Palmer, John Lennon, Priscilla Presley, Nancy Reagan, Nat King Cole, Edgar Allan Poe, and Richard Burton.

Procreation doesn't make you a dad; that title must be earned.

– AH

In May of 2005, I had a chance to go on a mission trip to *Bryansk, Russia*. Bryansk is a fairly large city roughly eight hours by train southwest of Moscow. The city's population is around 450,000 people and is primarily known for its cannon and munitions factories that were very active during and after the Second World War. It is lesser known for its close proximity to *Chernobyl.*

On April 26, 1986, reactor number four at the Chernobyl Nuclear Power Plant exploded unleashing a cloud of radioactivity over Western Russia, Ukraine, and Belarus that was four hundred times greater than the fallout released by the atomic bombing of Hiroshima during World War II. This radioactive devastation became more than just a news report or history lesson to me as we traveled through the dense forest that surrounds Bryansk. From about six feet down, all the bark on the trees looked normal: dark brown, almost black. But from six feet up, all the bark was a reddish orange color, not unlike the color of a summer sunset off the coast of Florida. It's as if someone had taken a level and drawn a perfectly straight line on the bark of every single tree, then smeared Georgia clay from that point to the peak of each one. It was the eeriest scene imaginable. That's when it hit me, "My God, how could anyone live through this? There's nowhere to go, no escape." Those that fled from the city to the forest couldn't escape their inevitable fate. Suddenly, quietly, my immediate future became crystal clear to me. We were going to take supplies to and visit with children in orphanages in Russia, all right; but more than that, we were about to deal with the babies of the children that almost twenty years earlier had survived a nuclear holocaust. The children that twenty years earlier had somehow survived that terrible time were now bearing children of their own.

When we reached our destination, we found that the orphanages were overflowing with happy children, but their laughter couldn't hide the physical deformities brought about by their parents' years of exposure to radiation. Only God knows what each child was dealing with inside both physically and mentally. But you know, kids are kids whether you're in Russia or Rhode Island, Finland or Florida, Africa or Alaska. They all share one basic human need: to give and receive love. Those kids in the orphanages didn't want us to leave. They didn't care about what we did for a living or about what bills we had waiting for us when we got back home. They didn't care about how much our jobs paid (or didn't pay). They didn't care about what kind of car we drove, how much gas cost per gallon, whether we played in a bowling league, or even what church we attended. All they cared about was here and now. They lived for the moment they could show and be shown love. By the time we made it to the third orphanage, I had to make myself go in. I was emotionally drained. I wanted to take them all back to the States with us. Those kids showed us all what unconditional love is. It broke my heart every time we had to leave them.

One little boy in particular was very special to me. His name was Sasha. He was probably around three, and as my best friend would say, "A live wire with no insulation"! He loved to play and show me all the special flips and jumps he could do. But I was never out of his line of sight, and he would quickly run back over to me and climb up in my lap. Even though we didn't speak the same language, we somehow managed to communicate through pointing and pictures. I still have a picture of him and often wonder how he's doing all these years later. So it is with your own children. When they're little, they don't care about the day-to-day trials you consider crisis. All they want is you! They just want to share with you what they've learned this day, watch you smile, then crawl up in your lap, feeling safe and secure knowing that you love and care for them. When they grow older and start to have problems of their own, they still need you, both of you. They deal with relationships both inside and outside the family unit, and boy do they deal with peer pressure. But guess what, even though you might not think so, they still want and need you. They want to share their knowledge with you, see you smile in approval, and then physically (if not figuratively) crawl up in your lap feeling safe and secure knowing that you love and care for them.

My adopted dad told me something when I was young that I have never forgotten, and it's especially meaningful to me because I was adopted. He said, "And no matter what you do in life, one thing will never change, you will *always* be my son." Wow. My dad is in his seventies now, and those words mean just as much to me today as they did almost fifty years ago. My dad isn't my dad because of biology, he earned the right to be called my dad because of love. He picked me out of all the other kids he saw and raised me as his own. I haven't always remembered that, and there were times when he must have wondered "What have I done?" but I love my parents for spending time with and raising me.

I believe that God gave women an extra portion of what we like to call *maternal instinct*, but hear me loud and clear, men, God never designed a family to be made up of children and a single parent. It's the role of the mother *and* father to raise, support, and protect their children. It's not the job of the grandparents or the government – it's the parents' job! Now common sense tells me that sometimes things happen beyond our control, and *occasionally*, the responsibility falls on others to take over; but in those instances, the family should step up first, and if that's not possible, then society should step in. Like I said in the very first chapter of this book, only about 63 percent of American children grow up with both biological parents, and that's a shame. Now I realize (validated through my research) that there are a lot of blended families out there, but the majority of them become blended because of divorce and remarriage. I know that there are real reasons for divorce too. But I'm not so dumb as to believe that a great majority of divorce happens because of true "irreconcilable differences." That's just another way of saying, "I'm selfish, and if things don't go the way I want them to, I'm outa here!"

Guys, consider what you're doing to your kids. What are you really saying to your children when you tell them that it's not their fault that you and mommy are getting divorced? That you still love them with all your heart, but you're just not in love with their mom anymore. Children trust your actions more than the words you say. Your actions tell them that you loved Mommy enough to marry her, have children with her, and be with her till death do you part. Well, that was a lie, and if that was a lie, then the love that you *say* that you have for them *with all of your heart* might just be a lie too. Again, I'm not so stupid as to think that all marriages are rosy and that they aren't some real hard-core reasons for divorce, but society has made it too easy and, quite frankly, socially acceptable to split up because things get tough or you don't get your way.

Step up, guys, be a man. Earn the right to be called dad. Be honest with yourself and consider the consequences of an unplanned pregnancy. Don't let a few (in some cases seconds) of pleasure determine your path for the rest of your life, but if it does, stand up. Don't put all the pressure and pleasure of raising a child solely on your wife, her parents, or anyone else. Be a part of your children's life. Help your wife feed the baby, change their diapers (I know, I know, but do as I say, not as I do), set boundaries, discipline with love, always back up your wife, show a united front, play ball or tea party with your kids, and above all remember that it's *your* responsibility as a father to raise your children.

You may have heard it said that "it takes a village to raise a child." Wrong mentality! What it takes is a dedicated, devoted mother and father who will love, support, and protect their children and each other. If every family practiced these, there wouldn't be the need for a village to step in.

In bringing up children, spend on them half as much money, and twice as much time.

– Author Unknown

Chapter 7

It's Okay to Be Number Two

Only a life lived for others is a life worthwhile.

– Albert Einstein

RELATIONSHIPS ARE SELDOM easy; they require a personal investment. And if time is not part of that investment, then the relationship withers and dies.

Not long ago I had a friend of mine asked me, "How are you going to end your book? How are you going to tie it all together?" I guess I could sum all this up in one word: *love*. In order for a marriage to work and last a lifetime, you have to love your wife with all your heart. No matter how life tries to get you sideways and put you in the ditch, remember that your wife loves you, warts and all. You're the same man you were the day you said "I do." You just need to keep reminding yourself that there is someone else besides you that is very, very important in your life. Trust me, contrary to what the world tells you, you don't need to be first all the time. The world tells you to look out for number one, so go ahead; but remember, as far as created things go, your wife should be number one in your life. The Bible says in 1 Corinthians 13:11, "When I was a child, I spoke as a child, I understood as a child, I thought as a child: but when I became a man, I put away childish things" (American KJV). You know, when I was a kid, I wanted things *my* way. I had *my* stuff. I did things that were beneficial to *me*. But when I grew up and got married, I realized that there was someone who I loved tremendously and was willing to put ahead of me. It wasn't about *me* anymore, it was about *us*. It was time for me to give up being childish, time to put on the "big-boy pants" and be a man. Putting someone else ahead of you in your life doesn't make you less of a man, it makes you a *better* man.

You know I've talked a lot about common sense. Common sense would tell you that the way you live your life physically the first forty or so years will have a huge impact on your last forty or so years (if you last that long). I didn't do such a good job the first forty years of my life. I ate all the wrong foods, and way too many of them. I was overweight and didn't exercise much. So between the ages of forty and fifty, I've struggled with diabetes, high blood pressure, and heart disease. But even though I haven't done a great job of listening to my wife, my family, or even my own body, Lisa has been beside me all the way. Through knee surgery, cancer surgery, and open heart surgery, she's taken care of me. She never threw her hands up, said "that's it, I'm done," or gave up on me. She has taught me the meaning of loyalty. I recall one time after a surgery, I wrote her a letter in which I told her that she deserved a life better than the one she shared with me. She wrote me a letter back and essentially said that I needed to get over myself. That in our vows we said "for better or worse." Vows she never took for granted. That this part of our lives was just a bump in the road, and if she had ever thought about ending our marriage, she would have never stayed married this long. (Kind of a backhanded compliment, but okay, I'll take it.)

I think our biggest trial came on August 19, 2003. Almost two years prior to that date I had my first heart attack. I blamed it on drinking bad milk. I had cold sweats, my left arm went numb, and my jaw hurt; but it was bad milk all the way (sure it was)! I kept telling myself that until the doctor that had performed my knee surgery was concerned that my legs were swollen and I wasn't healing as fast as he would like. So he recommended that I go see a cardiologist. I went in for my first round of *coronary artery*, or heart stents, a few weeks later. However, the body is a wonderfully complex thing; it's built so that it knows if there is foreign material trapped inside it, and it does it's best to get rid of whatever that material is. My body saw the stent as a threat, and as a good body should, it filled the inside of that tube (stent) with my own cells to protect me. The problem was that in filling up the stent, it reduced the size of the opening of my artery as time passed. Six months later, I was having the same symptoms as before. After about twenty months, three rounds of stents, and even radioactive seeds being used to keep the stents clear, things got progressively worse. The surgeon finally came to Lisa and me and said, "We can keep playing this game every six months, or we can go in, do bypass, and probably get you twenty years." For me that was a *no-brainer.* The surgeon wanted me to stay in the hospital, and they would do the surgery in a few days. I however had other plans. My plan (against Lisa's wishes) was to go home, get a lot of things organized at work, and do the surgery in about six weeks. Needless to say, things didn't work out the way I wanted. Within a few days, I was having chest pains and the same old problems. I called the cardiologist, and the next morning, we were headed for the hospital. I can't quite explain how it feels to have tubes down your throat, in your chest, and other places that hurt a whole lot worse. Lisa said that when she came to see me in the ICU recovery after the five-hour surgery, I literally looked dead. My skin was gray, and I was barely responsive. But she was right there. She's the fist person I remember talking to on my way to the recovery room. I was in the hospital almost a week surrounded by my family and friends, and Lisa was there every day, coaching me through my breathing treatments and warning me when the nurses from physical therapy were on their way (I hated physical therapy). For any spouse to have to go through this sort of trial with their loved one is exhausting, but our journey had just started. I had only been home about four days when my mom, who had been staying with us to help out after the surgery, noticed an infection in the incision in my chest. We contacted the surgeon's office, and after a quick office visit, I was back in the hospital, sequestered to a quarantined area of the second floor this time to have the whole incision debrided. That's when they have to cut out a section of both sides of the incision to make sure they get out all of the infected tissue. Now instead of a nice small zipper scar, I had a huge cavern where you could see down to the wires holding my sternum together. Now my recovery became even more complicated. Since the opening was so long and deep, special care had to be taken to clean and dress it. Rolls of gauze had to be soaked in a solution and then lightly packed into the opening. Then a large bandage had to be cut and taped over the gauze. The worst part was that every twelve hours, the bandage had to be removed, the old gauze taken out, and the procedure started all over again. I was lucky that I was able to have a home health care nurse come see me occasionally, and in the beginning, she showed Lisa how to perform the procedure. It took me six weeks before I could even look at the incision and the wires, but my wife, my friend, was there from day one to help me. For three and a half months, twice a day she changed those bandages and never complained. I'm not sure if the tables were turned if I would have the stomach to do the same, but I would definitely try. I know my wife loves me. She's proved it to me in not just the major things she's shown me, but in a million little ways that I almost forget about daily. I try to make it a point to tell her "thank you" for everything she does for me (when I remember), and I tell her I love her every day. Every single day at least a half a dozen times she hears me say the words. Words in themselves don't always mean that much, but I try to show her with my actions that she's the most important created thing to me. I love our son, Justin, and my family immensely, but Lisa will always be above them. The bond between a husband and wife should always come first. It really hurts me when I interview a previously divorced man who has remarried and tells me that his kids come first. That's not the way it's supposed to work. His marriage is practically doomed from the beginning if he doesn't put his wife's needs and desire for love above his children's. I know that's hard to hear. Hollywood and our culture of today tend to accept the fact that we should love our children more than our spouses, but it's awfully hard to keep a family intact when our wives feel neglected and end up somewhere way down the line on our "love list." Listen, when Justin was born and Lisa devoted more of her time to him instead of me, I felt jealous. Even though it was the right thing to do, I still wanted to be the primary man in her life. Those of you men whose wives have had kids, you know where I'm coming from. In Genesis 2:24, the Bible says that a man shall leave his father and his mother, and shall cleave (stick to) his wife, and the two shall become one. Nowhere does God say anything about a man and his children becoming one. This special union is only meant for a man and his wife. It all comes down to growing up and putting your spouse's wants and desires ahead of your own. Now I realize that no one is perfect. Even famous, important, respected men have a hard time with selflessness. Men like Bill Clinton, Jim Bakker, John Edwards, King David, Jimmy Swaggart, and Jesse Jackson all had problems with putting their spouse's feelings ahead of their own wants and childish desires. Infidelity is poison to a marriage and hard to recover from. Although forgiveness may happen early on, the regaining of trust always takes longer. Look, all of us make mistakes, but if what the Bible says is true, and if we and our wife are one, then who among us would intentionally hurt ourselves? Slow down; think before you do something stupid that your marriage may not recover from. Love your wife with all your heart and put her needs above your own.

When I was young, I used to stutter a lot. My dad worked with me to help me improve my speech and gave me some great words of wisdom that not only helped me with my stuttering, but also helped me later on in my marriage. It keeps me from saying stupid stuff all the time. His advice was to stop, think about what I was going to say, then say it. There were and are a lot of famous people who stutter. People like Moses, Aristotle, Lewis Carroll, Winston Churchill, Bruce Willis, James Earl Jones (yes, Mr. CNN, no kidding), Mell Tillis, Bo Jackson, Bill Walton, Marilyn Monroe, John Stossel, and Jimmy Stewart to name just a few. I'll bet you that most of them, somewhere along the way, figured out how to stop and think about what they were gonna say before they said it. This is a pretty easy skill to initiate, but a hard one to master. Before you speak, think about the impact your words might have. Words are like bullets fired from a gun; once they leave the barrel, there's no taking them back. Consider the ramifications your words might have on your wife, your children, or even your marriage. The words we choose to speak can either "tear down" or "build up." Choose to build.

While you've been reading this book, you may have thought to yourself, "Hey, something's a little off, there's something about the way this guy writes." Maybe you picked up on something while you were reading *between* the lines. Well, you were right. I guess it's time to come clean. Although I really don't have an MD, PhD, OG, or LMNOP after my name, I am a licensed, ordained Southern Baptist minister. I'm not ashamed of that at all, but I do realize that some people are turned off by religion. I wanted you to hear my heart before you made up your mind about this book, and me. I wanted you to know that whatever race, creed, color, or religion you are, marriage and the family are firm foundations we should all stand on as men and Americans.

A long time ago I had an old evangelist tell me something that has stuck with me for a lot of years, even though I haven't always heeded his advice. He told me that in my life I had to put God first, my wife second, my children third, and then the church – and not to ever get them out of order. He knew that God gave us our wives to help us, whether we asked for it or not. God gave us our wives to be our partners in this journey we call life. God gave us our wives to be our second conscience when we refuse to listen to our own.

In the last few pages of this book you'll find a sample of the survey that I used as a guide in my interview process. Take time to fill it out on your own. Look to see if anything you're doing right or wrong jumps out at you. When you're done, go over your answers with your wife, or wife-to-be. See if you're on the same page emotionally. We as men always have room for improvement when it comes to relationships, especially with our wives. Talk, talk, talk! Communication is the key to a better understanding of your spouse. Make your wife your best friend. Pick your battles. Understand that a marriage goes through phases. Remember that a woman goes through physical and emotional changes for most of her life. Keep her laughing; love and laughter go hand in hand. Don't make your wife a single parent; it takes a devoted mom *and* dad to raise children. Finally, the key word found in all long and successful marriages is "LOVE." Love means putting your wife ahead of you. Think of her wants and desires before you get your own way.

I hope that you've found something useful in the pages of this book, and if not useful, at least entertaining. Maybe you can learn from my experiences and mistakes. And those of other guys married a quarter of a century. Just remember the following:

There are three kinds of men. The one that learns by reading. The few that learn by observation. The rest of them have to pee on the electric fence for themselves.

– Will Rogers

Marriage Questionnaire

(For Men)

1. How old are you? _____
2. What race are you? _____
3. How long have you been married? _____
4. What month were you married in? _____
5. How long did you date before you got engaged? _____
6. How long were you engaged before you got married? _____
7. Have you been married before? _____
8. If yes, for how long? _____
9. What month did you get married in? _____
10. How long did you date before you got engaged? _____
11. How long were you engaged before you got married? _____
12. What caused the end of the previous marriage? Wife's death ____
    Divorce ____ Brief Reason _____
13. Any children from present marriage? _____
14. If yes, how many? Gender? _____
15. Any children from previous marriage(s)? _____
16. If yes, how many? Gender? _____
17. Does your blended family have children living with you? _____

Explain the arrangement.

_____
_____
_____

18. Are your parents still living? _____
19. If so, are they still married to each other? _____

20. If yes, for how long? _____

21. If not, what happened? _____

22. Are they remarried? _____ For how long? _____

23. Do you have any siblings? _____

24. Gender? Are they Married? _____ Divorced? _____
Re-married? _____ Single (never been married) _____

Other _____

25. Are your children married? _____ Divorced? _____

Remarried? _____ Single (never been married) _____

Other _____

26. How old were you when you married your present wife? _____

27. How old was your wife? _____

28. How old were you when you got married the first time? _____

29. How old was your wife? _____

30. Where were you married to your present wife? (Geographic location.)
_____

31. Previous wife? _____

32. Where were you and your present wife married? Church? _____

Justice of the Peace? _____ Other _____

33. Did your parents approve of your marriage? (Did they like your fiancé?)

Explain
_____
_____
_____

34. How often do you (without distractions) sit down and talk to your wife?

Every day _____ Couple times a week _____ Weekly _____

Occasionally _____ Hardly ever _____ Never _____

35. When was the last time? _____
36. What did you talk about? _____
37. When was the last time you and your wife had any argument?
_____
38. Has it been resolved? _____ How? _____
39. When was the last time you had a *serious* argument? _____
40. About what? _____
_____
41. How did you resolve it? _____
_____
42. What do you argue about the most? _____
43. What's the longest period of time you stayed mad after an argument? _____
44. As a rule, who apologizes first? _____
45. Do you apologize even when you're right? _____
46. What phrases do you use when you apologize? I'm sorry _____

Forgive me _____ Others _____

47. Have you ever brought up hurtful arguments from the past? ____
48. How did you feel after you said what you said? _____
_____
49. Do you have any religious affiliation? _____
50. With what religion? _____
51. Do you attend church on a regular basis? _____
    How often? _____
52. Does your wife have any religious affiliation?_____
53. Expound. _____
_____
54. Do (did) your parents have any religious affiliation? _____
55. Expound. _____
_____
56. Do your children have any religious affiliation? _____
57. Expound. _____
58. Do you know your wife's birthday? _____
59. Your anniversary? _____
60. Do you plan anything special for those days? _____
61. What's the nicest thing you've done for your wife on either day?
_____

62. Was it a surprise? _____ 63. Was she as excited as you were? _____
64. Do you do anything special for her any other time of the year?

_____

65. When? _____
66. What do you do? _____

_____

67. Does she like it when you buy her expensive things? _____
68. Does she like it more when you buy her less expensive, thoughtful gifts?

_____

Like:_____

69. On average, how much thought do you put into purchasing a Card? _____ Gift? _____
70. Has your wife ever returned a gift you got for her? _____
71. Expound. _____

_____

72. How did that make you feel? _____
73. Have you ever returned a gift your wife got you? _____
74. Expound. _____
75. Do you and your wife only have joint checking and savings accounts? _____
76. Do you have separate banking accounts? _____
77. Do you have both? _____ Expound. _____
78. Do you have separate credit cards (personal bills) as well as joint?

_____

79. Who handles the finances (paying the bills), and how is that done? (Does wife pay for her bills out of her account, and you pay for yours, etc.?)

_____

80. Do you or your wife have any type of allowance (any specific money set aside for you to spend on whatever you want)?

_____

81. Expound. _____
82. Have you ever written your wife a love note? _____
83. How often? _____ When was the last time?

_____

84. Do you ever leave her random notes (and where)? _____

85. How often? _____ When was the last time? _____

86. Has your wife ever had a major illness? _____

87. What, if anything, special did you do for her during her recovery?

_____

88. What, if anything, special did you do for her the last time she was sick?

_____

89. Does she do anything special for you when you're sick? _____

90. Expound. _____

91. Do you do any chores around the house? _____ What? _____

_____

92. Do you help with laundry? _____ Dishes? _____ Cooking? _____

93. How often do you tell her "Thank you"? Daily _____ 2-3 times a week _____

Weekly _____ Sometimes _____ Hardly ever _____

Never _____ Other _____

94. How often do you tell your wife you love her? _____

95. Do you have a special "date night" during the week? _____

96. What particular night is set aside as "date night"? _____

97. What do you do on "date night"? _____

98. When did you start having "date nights"? _____

99. How many times have you moved since you got married? _____

100. Do you still live in the same town you grew up in? _____

101. Do you live in the same town your wife grew up in? _____

102. Approximately how far do you live from your parents or nearest relative? _____

103. How far from your wife's parents or nearest relative? _____

_____

104. How far do you live from your children? _____

105. How many hours a week do you work? _____

106. What do you do for relaxation when you're not working? _____

107. What clubs or organizations do you belong to? _____

_____

108. How many nights per week are you away from home because of work?

5-7 _____ 4-6 _____ 2-3 _____ 1 _____ Hardly ever _____

Other _____

109. Expound. _____

110. How many nights are you away from home because of other reasons?

5-7 _____ 4-6 _____ 2-3 _____ 1 _____ Hardly ever _____

Other _____

111. Expound. _____

112. How many nights a week is your wife away from home? _____

113. Expound _____

114. What, if anything, would you change about your marriage (or wife)?
_____
_____

115. Who (or what) comes first in your life? _____Second?_____

Third? _____ Fourth? _____

www.ingramcontent.com/pod-product-compliance
Lightning Source LLC
Chambersburg PA
CBHW031329290526
45784CB00014B/2447